PREDATORS
HYENAS

Sally Morgan

RAINTREE
STECK-VAUGHN
RSVP PUBLISHERS

A Harcourt Company

Austin   New York
www.raintreesteckvaughn.com

LOOK FOR THE PREDATOR

Look for the hyena in boxes like this. Here you will find extra facts, stories, and other interesting information about hyenas.

Copyright Permissions
Steck-Vaughn Company
P.O. Box 26015
Austin, TX 78755

Published by Raintree Steck-Vaughn Publishers, an imprint of Steck-Vaughn Company

Library of Congress Cataloging-in-Publication Data

Cataloging-in-publication data is available at the Library of Congress.

ISBN 0-7398-6601-X

Acknowledgements
The Publishers would like to thank the following for permission to reproduce photographs:
CORBIS Corporation/Images: pages 3, 22 top. 25 top (Steve Kaufman), 31. Gallo Images/Anthony Bannister Photo Library: pages 1, 7 bottom, 28, 29 (Nigel J. Dennis); 2, 6, 10, 18, 19 bottom, 20, 21 bottom, 23, 30 (Clem Haagner); 4 (Richard du Toit); 5 top (Peter Chadwick); 7 top (Lorna Stanton); 8, 19 top (Martin Harvey); 9 top (Tim Jackson); 11 top (Alan Binks); 11 bottom, 13 left, 15 top (Anthony Bannister); 17 top (Wayne Saunders); 21 top (Wayne Griffiths); 22 bottom (Dave Hamman); 27 (Andrew Duthie). Frank Lane Photo Agency: pages 5 bottom (Gerard Laci); 9 bottom (Winifred Wisniewski); 12 (Minden Pictures); 13 right (Jurgen & Christine Sohns); 17 bottom (Peter Davey); 25 bottom (Martin Withers); 26 (W. Rohdich). Natural History Photo Agency: pages 14 (Ann & Steve Toon); 16, 24 (Jonathan & Angela Scott).
Cover photos: Front cover: CORBIS Corporation/Images.
Back cover: Ecoscene/Papilio/Pat Jerrold.

Printed in China/Hong Kong
07 06 05 04 03
10 9 8 7 6 5 4 3 2 1

CONTENTS

Laughing Scavenger 4

Killing Machine 6

Grassland Home 8

Hyena Food 10

Bone-crushing Grip 12

Hyena Senses 14

Going Hunting 16

In for the Kill 18

Learning to Kill 20

Enemies and Fighting 22

Under Threat 24

Hyena Facts 26

Hyena Words 28

Hyena Projects 30

Index 32

LAUGHING SCAVENGER

A strange cackling laugh is heard on the grassland. It is the call of the spotted hyena. This unusual sound has earned the spotted hyena the nickname "laughing hyena."

The hyena is both a predator and a scavenger. Predators are animals that hunt and eat other animals. The animals they hunt are called prey. Another name for a predator is carnivore, or meat-eater. A scavenger is an animal that feeds mostly on dead animals and plants.

▼ The spotted hyena got its name from the spots all over its body and legs.

◀ The brown hyena is smaller than the spotted hyena and has long shaggy fur.

▼ The aardwolf is an unusual looking animal. The word aardwolf is Afrikaans and it means "earth wolf." Aardwolves are called this because they dig dens or burrows in the ground.

The hyena belongs to the group of animals called mammals. Mammals produce milk to feed their young and have a body that is covered in hair. There are four species, or types, of hyena—the spotted, striped, and brown hyena, and the aardwolf. The spotted hyena is the largest and most common member of the hyena family. Although hyenas look like dogs, their closest relatives are mongooses, civets, and genets.

WHERE THEY LIVE

The spotted hyena (scientific name *Crocuta crocuta*) is found in west, east, and southern Africa. The aardwolf (*Proteles cristatus*) and the brown hyena (*Hyaena brunnea*) are found in southern Africa. The striped hyena (*Hyaena hyaena*) is found across North Africa, including Somalia, as well as in the Middle East, Turkey, Iran, Pakistan, and India.

KILLING MACHINE

In Africa there are more hyenas than any other large predator. They are excellent hunters, with with muscular shoulders and powerful jaws filled with bone-crushing teeth. They are also very smart animals.

▼ Hyenas have powerful jaws and can rip a carcass to pieces in a very short time.

One of the most obvious features of the spotted hyena is its compact head and thick neck. The neck leads to powerful shoulders and forelegs. The back slopes down to its hind legs. All hyenas have a mane of long hair that runs down the neck and back. The spotted hyena has a relatively small mane, but the hairs stick up, making it look larger.

HEAVY HYENA
The spotted hyena can weigh up to 176 pounds (80 kilograms), and the female is larger than the male. In contrast, the aardwolf weighs no more than 26 pounds (12 kilograms).

▶The large teeth of the spotted hyena are ideal for crushing bones.

Hyenas can travel very far. The brown hyena is known to travel 19 miles (30 kilometers) or more in a day. Hyenas have a lot of stamina or "staying power." They can run for hours at a time. They gallop at speeds of 25-30 miles (40-50 kilometers) per hour. Their top speed is about 37 miles (60 kilometers) per hour . A spotted hyena can maintain that speed for distances up to three miles (5 kilometers).

▼ The sloping back of the hyena is very obvious when viewed from the side.

GRASSLAND HOME

Hyenas live mostly on open grassland. Rain falls for only part of the year so the grass is often brown. After the rains the grassland turns a lush green.

The African grasslands are home to herds of grazing animals such as antelopes, gazelles, wildebeests, and zebras. These animals are all preyed on by the spotted hyena. Hyenas are social animals and they live together in family groups. The groups are called clans. Each clan lives in a particular area called a territory.

▼ In southern and eastern Africa, hyenas are found on the flat grasslands, called the savanna, alongside zebras and other large mammals.

SEARCHING FOR FOOD
The brown hyena is found in the Kalahari Desert of southwest Africa. Very few animals live in the desert, so there is little food for the hyena. A brown hyena may spend ten hours each day just looking for food.

The territory has to be large enough for the hyenas to find all the food and water they need. Members of the clan patrol the boundaries of their territory and defend it against intruding clans. The spotted hyena lives in territories of up to 15 square miles (390 square kilometers). This is about half the size of Manhattan. The brown hyena has territories that are even larger. The members of a clan rear their young together in a central place within their territory known as the den. Here there are underground tunnels where the youngsters can be raised and hidden from other predators.

▲ These spotted hyenas are patrolling their territory.

▼ A hyena's den is usually found on high ground in the central part of the territory. The above-ground entrances are connected to a series of underground tunnels.

HYENA FOOD

Spotted hyenas are skilled hunters. As well as hunting prey, hyenas scavenge for food. They will eat almost any food left untouched by other animals. For this reason, the hyena has been described as a master scavenger.

The spotted hyena hunts large prey such as zebras, wildebeests, and other large mammals. It will also steal from other predators, for example, leopards, lions, and African wild dogs. The smaller brown and striped hyenas are mainly scavengers, but they will catch small mammals, lizards, and insects. The aardwolf is a shy animal that hunts mostly at night. It feeds on termites, which it licks up using its long, sticky tongue.

MEAT FEAST

A spotted hyena can eat as much as 33 pounds (15 kilograms) of meat, which it swallows extremely quickly.

▼ Hyenas will eat almost all of a kill, including the bones and skin.

The digestive system of a hyena can cope with almost any food. It can even digest bone. Hyenas' powerful teeth can crack open the largest of bones. Then they swallow the pieces of bones. Any food that cannot be digested after it has been swallowed—hooves and hair, for example —are vomited up and spat out as pellets.

Spotted hyenas will steal food from lions as well as killing their own prey. Vultures wait for any leftovers.

► The aardwolf hunts at night when termites emerge from their nests.

BONE-CRUSHING GRIP

The most important weapons of the spotted hyena are its jaws and teeth. Its jaws are among the most powerful of any predator.

The pointed teeth near the front of the jaws are the canines, which are used to stab prey. The large teeth behind the canines are for crushing bones. The teeth at the back of the jaws are adapted to cutting through skin and crushing bones. A thick muscular neck and powerful shoulders support the hyena's compact head. The hyena grips its prey with its teeth and uses its neck and shoulders to pull the victim to the ground.

ANCIENT TEETH

It is thought that hyenas grew their special teeth to cope with eating the tough remains of kills left by the saber-toothed cats. Saber-toothed cats lived two million years ago.

▼ A spotted hyena opens its jaws wide, showing its large, curving canines and the bone-crushing teeth behind them.

▲ A young spotted hyena uses its eyes and ears to find prey. Hyenas also listen for the sounds of animals being killed by other predators.

The smaller hyenas have less powerful jaws and smaller teeth. They cannot kill large prey. Instead they hunt smaller prey such as insects, lizards, and small mammals. The aardwolf has an even smaller jaw with peglike teeth.

◄ The brown hyena is much smaller than the spotted hyena and eats much smaller prey.

HYENA SENSES

Hyenas use their senses to find food and to communicate with each other. The most important senses are hearing, sight, and smell.

Hyenas patrol the boundaries of their territory. They place scent marks along the boundaries. Their bodies can produce a strong smelling substance, which they smear over long stalks of grass at nose height. Other hyenas cannot miss the smell as they walk nearby.

▼ Hyenas have good eyesight and use it to locate one another at a distance. Close up, they communicate more by sounds and smell.

This adult hyena is sniffing a blade of grass that has been marked by another hyena. The scent mark has a strong odor.

Members of a clan need to be able to recognize one another. When two hyenas meet, they sniff each other. Hyenas keep in contact when they are hunting or roaming around in search of food by using sound. They produce a range of sounds including whoops, yells, giggles, and cackles. These sounds can travel many miles over the grassland. Hyenas produce a high cackling laugh when they are being chased, are frightened, or get particularly excited.

Hyenas eat a lot of bones, so their droppings are chalky white. Members of a clan leave their droppings in the same places, which are called latrines. The latrines act as territory markers.

HOWLING HYENAS
When a hyena wants to make contact with other members of the clan, it tilts its head slightly toward the ground and produces a long drawn-out howl.

GOING HUNTING

Hyenas hunt mostly from dusk to dawn. They tend to prey on young, old, or diseased animals, rather than fit and healthy animals. By removing the weaker individuals of herds of grazing animals, hyenas allow other herd members to roam freely.

▼ Small animals such as this gazelle are easy prey for the spotted hyena.

HANGING ON

The jaws of a hyena are so strong that it can hang from the throat of an animal and completely lift itself off the ground. A hyena was once seen leaping more than six feet (two meters) to reach meat hanging from a tree. The hyena seized the meat and remained hanging there. A second hyena leapt up and sank its teeth into the leg of the first hyena. The jaws of the first hyena had to support not only its own weight but also the weight of the hanger-on.

The spotted hyena usually hunts alone, but it may be joined by others of its clan. It is strong enough to pull down a large animal on its own. It can also keep up a steady speed over long distances. For example, it can chase a wildebeest for several miles without tiring. When necessary a hyena can run at speeds of up to 37 miles (60 kilometers) per hour.

Spotted hyenas often work together in small groups when they are hunting zebras. The hunt starts off with one or two hyenas. They run toward a herd and get the zebras running. Then they pick out their target. Often this will be an animal that is weaker than the others. As many as 10 or 15 hyenas may join in the chase, which can last several miles. About one in every three of these chases ends with a successful kill.

▲ These hyenas have grouped together, ready to join in the chase for a large mammal.

▼ The spotted hyena is a powerful predator. It can run down and kill a wildebeest that is more than three times its own weight.

IN FOR THE KILL

Hyenas are powerful animals and efficient hunters, but they do not kill their prey quickly. Once a group of hyenas has surrounded their prey, they kill it by pulling it to pieces.

The hyena normally seizes its prey by the leg and hangs on until the animal falls to the ground. Then it tears off the soft flesh between the hind legs and on the belly. Usually the prey is dead within five to ten minutes. As many as 50 hyenas may cluster around the kill. They eat the flesh, skin, and bones as quickly as possible. A group of hyenas can completely pull a zebra to pieces and eat it in 15 minutes.

▼ Spotted hyenas have to eat their meals in one sitting or other predators and scavengers may arrive and steal some of their food.

EGG THIEF
A brown hyena was once seen removing and hiding 26 eggs from an ostrich nest, one by one. It came back later to eat them.

The hyenas fight over the kill and they make a lot of noise. This attracts other predators such as lions and wild dogs. Vultures, too, will come down to scavenge some food. If the kill takes place near the boundary of two territories, a rival clan may appear, attracted by the noise. This leads to fighting in which hyenas may be injured or even killed.

Brown and striped hyenas may be chased away from their food by larger predators such as lions and cheetahs. When they find a large amount of food, they may hide some of it and come back later to eat it. They usually return at night, when the larger predators are sleeping.

▼ These spotted hyenas will quickly pull the body of the hippopotamus to pieces.

▲ Hyenas will eat eggs. Here a hyena is trying to break open the tough shell of an ostrich egg.

LEARNING TO KILL

Hyena cubs are born in underground tunnels. They have teeth and their eyes are open at birth. Unlike other predators, they can walk right away. They fight with their brothers and sisters from a very young age.

For the first few weeks, the baby hyenas stay with their mother. Then she moves them to another tunnel to be with all the other youngsters. The hyena cubs drink milk from their mother for many months. A few of the hyena cubs may start to eat meat at three months old, but most will not do so until they are at least eight months. Some of the youngsters may still be taking milk when they are over one year old.

▼ This young hyena cub is watching how an adult crushes a bone with its teeth.

DANGEROUS GAMES

Play fights between cubs can be serious and as many as one cub in four may be killed by another cub.

◄ These two young cubs will probably spend much of the day playing with each other. The rough and tumble of play helps hyena cubs develop the skills they will need to hunt and fend off enemies.

The cubs play with each other. They are not afraid to use their teeth, and some of their fights can lead to cubs being injured. The cubs will also play with sticks and stones. Once the cubs are one year old, they will follow their mother on her hunting and scavenging trips. Until then they are left behind at the den with an adult.

The cubs of the aardwolf are weaned (eat food instead of milk) much earlier. By the time they are three months old, they will accompany a parent to learn how to find termite nests. They have to learn to listen for the sounds of termites eating and how to lick up termites using their tongue.

▲ By the time an aardwolf is four months old, it is ready to spend much of the night alone, hunting for termites.

ENEMIES AND FIGHTING

Hyenas are not the only predators on the grassland. They have to compete with other predators for food.

One of the biggest threats comes from lions. Lions hear the noisy giggling of hyenas around a kill, and they soon come to investigate. A single lion may not be able to chase off a group of hyenas, but the arrival of a pride of lions will frighten the hyenas away. The hyenas retreat to a safe distance and wait for the lions to eat their fill. Then they will creep back to finish off the bones and other remains. At other times, it is the hyenas that chase lions from a kill.

▲ By showing its killing teeth, a hyena will often deter any would-be attacker.

▼ African wild dogs and spotted hyenas often fight over a kill.

Competition also comes from the African wild dog. The wild dogs live in groups called packs. Just like the hyena, the wild dogs hunt together and they live in dens. If a pack of wild dogs comes across a single hyena near their den or near a kill, they will chase it and possibly attack it.

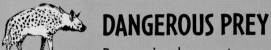

DANGEROUS PREY

Prey animals may turn on their attackers. An oryx antelope can kill a hyena that is chasing it by stabbing the hyena with its long pointed horns.

◀ Two lions are surrounded by a group of hyenas. The hyenas will move closer and closer and try to scare the lions away from their kill.

UNDER THREAT

Hyenas are one of Africa's most common predators. But in recent years, the numbers of hyenas have fallen considerably. This is due to both loss of habitat and hunting.

The number of people living in Africa is growing rapidly. People are moving into new areas and keeping sheep, cattle, and goats on land that was once grassland. This means that hyenas, along with many other animals, are losing their habitat. This is causing hyena populations to die out in some places.

The numbers of striped and brown hyenas have fallen so much that these hyenas are now classified as being endangered. This means that these species of hyena may become extinct in the future if nothing is done to save them.

SHARING MEALS
Striped and brown hyenas will often share a carcass, so they are better able to cope with limited food than the spotted hyena is.

▲ This Spotted hyena has been killed by lions.

In the past farmers believed that aardwolves killed their livestock so the farmers shot them. Aardwolves were also killed for meat and for their skin. However, aardwolves are useful animals as they eat lots of termites. Termites are serious pests that damage buildings. Today fewer aardwolves are shot. If aardwolves are conserved, there will be much better control of termites.

▼ This is an endangered striped hyena and her cub.

▼ Hyena cubs may be left alone when the mother goes to hunt, leaving them open to predators.

HYENA FACTS

Here is a selection of interesting facts about hyenas.

CAT-LIKE ORIGINS

The ancestors of hyenas appeared on Earth more than 26 million years ago. They looked like present-day civets, which are catlike mammals with a dark body and long tail. Civets are predators, too, coming out at night to hunt. The earliest fossil hyenas are found in Europe and Asia. Their skulls have the characteristic bone-crushing teeth.

MAGICAL POWERS

Hyenas are believed to have magical powers, and many people fear them for this reason. Some African cultures believe that witches can turn themselves into hyenas. This is similar to old European stories of black cats being linked to witches.

CHILDREN CATCHERS

Occasionally hyenas attack people and even kill them. Some villagers in Africa believe these people-eating hyenas are kept and fed by humans, who send them out on magical missions to catch children.

▶ **A black cat is thought to have supernatural powers. People in Africa consider the hyena to have similar mystical skills.**

CLAN MEMBERS

Hyenas have a complex social arrangement. A clan is lead by the top female hyena. She is called the alpha female and she will lead the hunt and be the first to eat at a kill. In the clan the females outrank the males and tend to be far more aggressive than the males. There are fights between individuals in the clan to win higher positions.

▼ Scientists can tell the health of hyenas in the wild by examining their teeth. Clean, undamaged teeth like these show the hyena is fit and healthy.

HUNTING HYENAS

The striped hyena is smaller than the spotted hyena and far more timid. The ancient Egyptians used to tame striped hyenas and use them for hunting. Some were fattened up and killed for meat.

SCENT FRENZY

During the mating season the aardwolf goes into a scent-marking frenzy. During this period one animal may leave as many as 120 marks in just two hours.

HYENA WORDS

This glossary explains some of the words used in this book that you might not have seen before.

Adapted
well suited to the surroundings.

Canine
large pointed tooth near the front of the mouth. A hyena has four canines, two in the top jaw and two in the lower jaw.

Carnivore
an animal that hunts and eats other animals—also known as a meat-eater.

Gorge
to eat a lot of food quickly.

Habitat
the place where an animal or plant lives, for example on the savanna or in a rain forest.

Mammal
a type of animal that produces milk for its young. Mammals have a body covered in hair.

Patrol
to walk or run around an area to guard or protect it.

Predator
an animal that hunts other animals and eats them.

▼ The spotted hyena is a highly intelligent predator.

▲ These young hyena cubs rely on their mother for all their food for the first year of their lives.

Prey
an animal that is hunted and killed by another animal—a predator—for food.

Savanna
tropical grassland found in eastern and southern Africa, where there are dry seasons and rainy seasons. Hyenas live mostly in grassland areas.

Scavenger
an animal that feeds on dead and decayed bodies of animals.

Termite
an insect that looks like a large ant and that lives in colonies of several millions.

Territory
the area of land in which an individual or group of individuals lives and often defends against others.

Weaned
stage in a young mammal's life when it starts eating solid food and stops taking milk from its mother.

HYENA PROJECTS

If you want to find out more about hyenas, here are some ideas for projects.

WATCHING HYENAS

Until recently very little was known about the hyena. Today, we still do not know much about the brown and striped hyenas. Our knowledge of these animals comes from people who spend many years watching them in the wild. Not everyone can see hyenas in the wild, but you may be able to visit a zoo or an animal park that keeps hyenas. Take a notebook with you and make notes of what you observe. For example, watch where the hyenas walk. Do they mark the boundaries of their enclosure? How do they greet each other? Do they sniff each other or rub heads?

WHAT EATS WHAT?

Starting with hyenas, draw a food chain for some of the wildlife on the grasslands of Africa. A food chain is a diagram linking each animal with the animals or plants it feeds on. The text in this book will give you some of the "links" in the hyenas' chain. To find more links, look at other books in your local library or look at some of the Internet sites listed opposite. See how many food-chain links you can make. Do any other African predators have similar animals and plants in their food chains? If so, how does this affect hyenas?

◀ **This spotted hyena cub sits with its mother.**

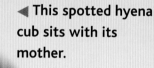

▲ Spotted hyenas are always alert for danger or fresh prey.

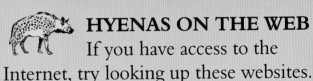

HOW YOU CAN HELP

Scientists who study hyenas in the wild and help protect them from habitat destruction and hunting need support for their work. Join a conservation group to find out more about hyenas and how you can help them survive. You will find details of these organizations on the Internet. Some conservation groups produce books, videos, and CDs about hyenas and other endangered wildlife. Many zoos have plans that allow you to "adopt" animals such as hyenas and help to pay for their upkeep.

HYENAS ON THE WEB

If you have access to the Internet, try looking up these websites.

African Wildlife Foundation
www.awf.org
This website has information on a wide range of African animals, including hyenas. There is information on conservation projects, too.

Seaworld
www.seaworld.org/AnimalBytes/hyenaab.html
Seaworld has an animal information database covering many different animals including the hyena. You can find a fact sheet on the hyena at this website.

Namib Brown Hyena Project
www.strandwolf.org.za
Website that gives information about a research project that is taking place in Namibia, looking at brown hyenas. The site has plenty of photos and latest news of the research project.

INDEX

aardwolf 5, 10, 13, 21, 24, 25, 27
antelopes 8, 23

bones 11, 12, 15, 18, 20, 22
brown hyena 5, 7, 8, 9, 10, 13, 19, 24, 30, 31

canines 12, 28
carnivores 4, 28
cheetahs 19
civets 5, 26
clans 8, 9, 15, 16, 19, 27
communication 14–15
cubs 20, 21, 29

dens 5, 9, 23
desert 8
digestion 11, 30
droppings 15, 30

ears 13
eggs 19
eyes 13, 20

females 26, 27
fights 19, 27
food and feeding 4, 8, 9, 10–11, 14, 18, 19, 22, 30

gazelles 8, 16
grassland 4, 8–9, 22, 24, 29

habitat loss 24, 31
head 6, 12
hippopotamus 19
howling 15
hunting 4, 11, 15, 16–17, 21, 22, 24, 25, 27, 31

injury 21, 23
insects 10, 13

jaws 6, 12, 13, 16, 28

latrines 15
laugh 4
legs 4, 5, 6, 18
leopards 10
lions 10, 11, 19, 22, 23
lizards 10, 13

magical powers 26
mammals 5, 8, 10, 13, 29
manes 6
milk 5, 20, 29
mother 20, 21, 25, 29

play 21

predators 4, 6, 9, 19, 22, 24, 29
prey 3, 4, 10, 18, 23, 29

savanna 8, 29
scavengers 4, 10, 18, 21
scent marks 14, 15, 27
senses 14–15
sight 14
smell 14
social groups 8, 27
sounds 15
speed 7, 16
spotted hyena 2, 3, 4, 7, 8, 9, 10, 13, 16, 17, 18, 22, 27, 30, 31
striped hyena 5, 10, 19, 24, 25, 27, 30

teeth 6, 7, 12, 13, 20, 21, 26, 28
termites 11, 21, 25, 29
territories 8, 9, 14, 19, 29

vultures 19

weight 6
wild dogs 10, 19, 22, 23
wildebeest 8, 10, 16, 17

zebra 8, 10, 17, 18